Abraham Meyer

Abraham Meyer was born in 1978 in Dusseldorf, Germany. He graduated from Cologne University with a degree in finance in 2000. From 2001 to 2008, he worked for Deutsche Bank. And 2008 – 2012 at Cologne Capital Asset Advisory. Since 2012 Abraham is an independent investment consultant, an investor.

In 2014 he became acquainted with the cryptocurrency and bought 100 Bitcoins. From that moment he recommends to all his clients when drawing up an investment portfolio of at least 10%, to invest in cryptocurrencies. He believes that crypto-currencies are the future of finance, and Bitcoin is Digital Gold.

I0465348

The cost of one Bitcoin is selected to $ 7800. The total market capitalization of all crypto-currencies recently exceeded $ 190 billion. Leading developers of graphics processors AMD and NVIDIA are preparing to release graphics cards optimized for mining.

If you still have no idea what the cryptocurrency is and why it is so noisy, then this book will help you understand that it will soon change the world we are familiar with.

For those who have just encountered technology, this book will help you understand the basics and take the first steps to buying, selling and storing Bitcoin and other cryptocurrencies.

Also, the book will help to make up your investment portfolio and participate in the ICO.

At the end of the book a whole list of useful services and sites that are regularly used by professional investors.

We want to note that this book is not an investment adviser and has only an informational nature.

Table of Contents

1. Cryptocurrency - what is it?

Cryptocurrency is a digital currency protected by cryptographic technologies. There is no physical analog to these monetary units, they exist only in virtual space.

Satoshi Nakamoto presented the concept of a fully decentralized electronic money system on October 31, 2008, in the article "Bitcoin: a peer-to-peer e-cash system" on the mailing list about cryptography. Despite numerous variants of assumptions, it is still unknown who is behind this pseudonym - a person or a group of people.

In early 2009, Satoshi Nakamoto released the first version of Bitcoin- wallet and launched the Bitcoin network. The cryptocurrency has several significant advantages.

First, inflation is not terrible for it. If the printing press goes mad and prints a large amount of paper money, it is logical that this money will depreciate. With bitcoins, this situation is excluded because in the bitcoin code, there is a limit on the extraction of 21 million bitcoins.

Another plus is decentralization. There is no single center from which the system is managed, which means that it is extremely difficult to disrupt the operation of this system by forcefully limiting the spread of currency. The network simply does not have a single owner; it is controlled by users around the world.

The next advantage is anonymity. You can track transactions and see how many bitcoins have moved from one wallet to another, but it is extremely difficult to determine who exactly the wallet's rightful owner. Any person can open a Bitcoin account. This requires appropriate software and Internet access.

The most surprising thing is that "non-existent" money in the real world has purchasing power. But the fact remains that it can be exchanged for goods and services in the same way as bills or coins that are in your wallet.

Crypto currency can be exchanged even for euros or dollars at your discretion. In many countries, people buy real estate, tickets, and gadgets in bitcoins, pay utilities for them or buy coffee, even Microsoft accepts bitcoins.

There is an interesting case, in 2013, one user of the forum dedicated to the bitcoins offered to exchange 10,000 bitcoins for a couple of pizzas. Another user agreed, ordered a pizza and got him a bitcoins for a wallet. So, the first user bought two pizzas for 10,000 bitcoin, a quantity of the cryptocurrency that is now worth more than $21 million.

In the US, because of problems with determining the legal status of the cryptocurrency, business with the exchange of bitcoins for goods or services is more complicated, so, first of all, it is necessary to consider cryptocurrency as an investment option. At the moment the game is definitely worth the candle: the bitcoin course is growing steadily. The most profitable investments are connected with the highest level of risk, so choose what is more important for you - an opportunity to make good money or complete peace of mind.

2. What is Bitcoin?

Bitcoin is «digital cash». This is simultaneously a digital currency and an online payment system. In this system, data encryption technologies provide control over the generation of monetary units and confirmation of the transfer of funds. The system works independently of the state central banks.

Bitcoin is the first and largest decentralized cryptocurrency. Other cryptocurrencies, which are not more than one hundred, are called altcoins. But it was the bitcoin that became the standard and it has the largest capitalization.

Bitcoins are created as a reward for performing mathematical calculations. The process of creating new blocks is called mining.

Users provide their computing resources for verifying addresses and recording transactions in the registry and are rewarded with a commission for the transaction and newly created bitcoins.

At first, it was relatively easy to create blocks, and the lone miners did it. Over time, the complexity grew, for mining required solid computing power, so the miners began to unite in pools and to extract new bitcoins from joint efforts.

It is easy to get confused in terms because the words "bitcoin" and "block" can designate any of the three parts of the concept: the basic block-technology, the protocol and the client that ensure the execution of transactions, and the actual cryptocurrency (money).

3. What is Blockchain?

A blockchain is a multifunctional and multilevel information technology designed for the reliable accounting of various assets. The bitcoin network consists of interrelated transaction blocks. Each subsequent block contains information about the previous one so that it is possible to build them into a single chain and obtain information about all previous transactions (but not about the owners of bitcoins).

Its main difference and the undeniable advantage is that this registry is not stored in any one place. Any user of this network can have a free registry. Digital records are combined into "blocks", which are then linked cryptographically and chronologically into a "chain" using complex mathematical algorithms. Each block is associated with the previous one and contains a set of records. New blocks are always added strictly to the end of the chain.

The encryption process, known as hashing, is performed by a large number of different computers running on the same network. If, as a result of their calculations, they all receive the same result, the block is assigned a unique digital signature (signature). As soon as the registry is updated and a new block is formed, it can no longer be changed. Thus, it is impossible to forge it. You can only add new entries to it. It is important to consider that the registry is updated on all computers on the network at the same time. Access to the current version of the registry makes it transparent to all participants.

Potentially, this technology covers all spheres of economic activity without exception and has many fields of application. Among them: finance, economics, and cash settlements, as well as operations with tangible assets (real property, real estate, cars, etc.) and intangible assets (voting rights, ideas, reputation, intentions, medical data, personal information, etc.).

Now, in order to conclude a normal deal, you need to go to a lawyer or a notary, pay and wait for the documents to be issued. Smart contracts work like vending machines: you simply throw bitcoin into the machine (that is, in the registry), and the contract kept by a third party, driver's license or any other service that you ordered falls into your account.

In addition, unlike traditional agreements, smart contracts not only contain information about the parties' obligations and penalties for their violation but also automatically ensure the fulfillment of all the terms of the contract.

Smart contracts allow you to exchange money, property, shares or other assets without recourse to intermediaries.

At a recent blockade summit in Washington, Vitalik Buterin, a 23-year-old programmer from the Ethereum project, explained that in an intelligent contract, an asset or currency is transferred to a program that monitors compliance with the set of conditions.

At some point, this program confirms that the fulfillment of the terms of the contract and automatically determines whether the specified asset should go to one of the participants in the transaction or immediately return to another participant (and perhaps the conditions are somewhat more complicated). All this time the document is stored and duplicated in the decentralized registry, which ensures its reliability and does not allow any of the parties to change the terms of the agreement.

For example, an intelligent thermoregulation system can transmit power consumption data to an intelligent electrical network. If you consume a certain amount of electricity, another chain of units automatically transfers the required amount from your account to the account of the energy company. As a result, the operation of the meter and the billing process are automated.

A doctor or patient can transfer their private key to a medical device, for example, a blood sugar monitor. Then this device can automatically record the patient's blood sugar values, observing safety requirements, and then, for example, exchange data with an insulin injection device that will automatically maintain the normal level of this blood parameter on the basis of this data.

You can also use this approach to control the use of intellectual property by determining how many times a user can access, share, or copy information. It can also be used to create voting systems with protection from falsifications, the dissemination of information without censorship restrictions and much more.

Using smart contracts, you can simply work in many areas of life, including logistics, management, law and even in elections.

4. What is the value of cryptocurrency?

Bitcoins are valuable because they are accepted as payment.

When we say that the currency is secured by gold, we mean that there is a place where you can exchange currency for gold. Bitcoin was originally not provided with anything, but with its spread, people began to exchange real goods for this cryptocurrency, thanks to the possibility of instant payment.

In a sense, they can say that bitcoin is provided by the price that a seller set for goods, i.e. the seller's promise to exchange goods for a certain amount of currency.

Bitcoin, as well as pound, euro, and dollar has value only in exchange for something, and no value in use. If everyone suddenly stops taking pounds, dollars, euros or bitcoins, the bubble will burst, and their value will drop to zero. But this is unlikely to happen: even in Somalia, where the government disappeared 20 years ago, Somali shillings are still accepted as payment.

5. How is the cryptocurrency produced and what are the algorithms for confirming its value?

The confirmation/consensus algorithm is a method for the gradual extraction of the cryptocurrency, which all the network participants agreed in advance.

What is the essence?

- To use the coin, and it grew in price, the following conditions are necessary:

- restriction in quantity;

- gradual extraction;

- the cost of resources for production (which is difficult to get is always appreciated);

- it has a unique technology or solves an unresolved problem so far (anonymity, fast payments, free or cheap transactions, security, lack of regulators).

5.1. Who are the miners? What is the benefit of mincing and servicing the block?

Miners are computer boards that create new blocks in the network for the sake of mining bitcoins. Miners using the resources of their computers find/create new blocks in the blockchain + fill these blocks with transactions of users of the network receiving a double benefit:

1. Having found/creating a new block, they get 12.5 bitcoins from it.

2. If the number of transactions is too high, network users are willing to pay a commission to the miners to ensure that their payments are included in the new block first. The commission depends on the number of transactions, the size of the block (now 1 MB) and the size of your transaction - it is constantly changing

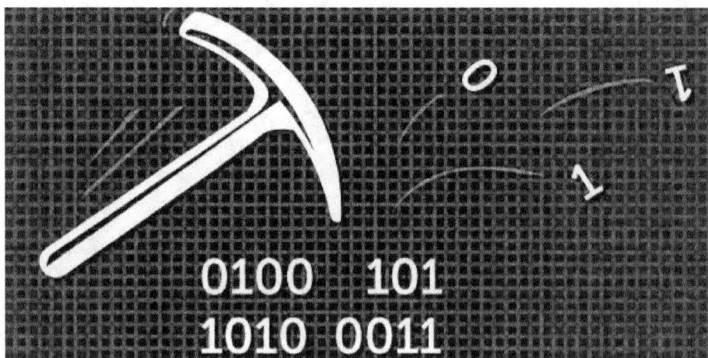

In this case, it is advantageous for the miners to fill the existing block more quickly, in order to start producing the next block sooner than the others. Whoever first finds a new block, he gets 12.5 bitcoins. Therefore, less powerful miners combine into mining pools to increase the chance of

finding blocks by them and then divide the output by the proportionately expended resource of each mining-pool participant.

5.2 What are the consensus algorithms?

Proof of Work - we spend resources in the form of electricity, time and purchase of special computer cards for finding new blocks and bitcoins in them. Example: Bitcoin

Problem/benefit: A lot of resources and electricity are spent; there is a risk of decentralization of 51% in the hands of 1 miner.

Proof of Stake - the more we hold the coins in the account, the greater the chance that we will find the next unit, while the wallet should be connected to the 24/7 network or you can rent the hosting.

Problem/benefit: A lot of resources and electricity are spent; there is a risk of decentralization of 51% in the hands of 1 miner.

Proof of Importance – the algorithm is similar to the Proof of Stake, but in addition to the presence of a coin on the account, it takes into account how long the coins lie in the wallet + how much and how many transactions you have spent with this currency. The more transactions you spend with the currency inside the network the more your reputation grows, which affects the passive mining of new coins. Example: NEM.

Problem/benefit. It allows us to avoid the decentralization and evenly distribute new coins between all active network members, for true coin fans.

Proof of Activity is a standard hybrid scheme combining PoW and PoS. Example: Dash.

Problem/benefit: We made a pre-fixing by determining the initial value of the coin and switched to a more sparing algorithm.

Delegated Proof of Stake is a general term describing the evolution of basic consensus-based protocols on the basis of share confirmation. Example: BitShares.

Proof of Burn — "Burning" occurs by sending coins to an address from which it cannot be guaranteed to be spent. Getting rid of their coins in this way, the user gets the right to lifetime mining, which is also arranged as a lottery among all owners of burnt coins.

Proof of Capacity is an implementation of the popular idea "megabytes as resources." It is necessary to allocate a significant amount of disk space to join the mining.

Proof of Storage - similar to the previous concept, in which the allocated space is used by all participants as a shared cloud storage.

6. What are the types of bitcoin earnings?

Without Investment:

1. Bitcoin-cranes or "faucets" (see advertising and get a penny): https://goo.gl/cEUoVG

2. Bounty (distribution of coins for social activity: translations, badges, signature, video, articles): https://bitcointalk.org/index.php?board=159.0

3. Affiliate Programs and Referrals: https://goo.gl/mtMTZP

4. Creating bots to exchange bitcoins.

5. Start accepting payments in bitcoins for your goods or services.

With the investment of funds:

1. Mining PoW - generate new blocks for the transaction we get in the form of commission bitcoins or another algorithm, for example, PoS

2. Rental of equipment in a mining pool: https://blockchain.info/pools

3. Trading (we trade in currency pairs): https://poloniex.com/exchange#btc_xmr

4. ICO – redemption of coins: https://tokenmarket.net/ico-calendar

5. Hypes and pyramids with bitcoins: https://goo.gl/JZFokG

6. Purchasing of master-nodes servicing the network

7. Creating your own exchange cryptocurrencies and earnings on a percentage of each transaction or exchanger.

7. What are nodes and master-nodes?

Node is a wallet that is not fully synchronized (more than 100 GB) with a block of the network.

Full Nodes (they are also full nodes of the network) are fully synchronized with the block of wallets that are connected to the network 24/7. Their function is to store all information about the network + to check whether new transactions are in line with the network rules, confirming or rejecting them when trying to include a transaction in new blockers. **Full nods work for free on the enthusiasm of the owners of** wallets!

Miners are computer boards that create new blocks in the network for the sake of extracting bitcoins + including new transactions confirmed by the nodes.

Master-nodes are fully synchronized wallets that are connected to the network 24/7. Their function is to serve the network, starting from conducting transactions and ending with additional services, such as providing complete anonymity of transactions (transactions are NOT written in the block, for example, in Dash), etc. depending on the technology of individual master codes.

Since master nodes are in fact partially performing the work of transaction processing miners, they take some of the found coins in a new block to themselves thus dividing the profits with the miners.

Should I freeze my capital by investing in a masterwork?

Not always, the risk ratio of the deposit amount in the master course and the monthly profit is usually very high, but the prospects for growth of coins with this technology are attractive!

8. Cryptocurrency storage

People who have decided to convert their savings into a cryptocurrency (exchange electronic money) or engage in earnings of cryptocurrency, immediately ask themselves where to store the cryptocurrency and how to choose a reliable wallet.

Without such storage, the accumulation or use of an alternative monetary unit is impossible, because, it does not have a material embodiment, exists and develops on the Internet.

- Separate wallets for each cryptocurrency

You can install a separate wallet on your computer. This approach undoubtedly provides a safe way to store digital currencies, because each of these wallets gives you the ability to control the private key. If the latter is stored in a secure place (for example, written on paper and/or stored on a flash device that is always offline), then you can be 100% sure of the safety of digital savings.

However, this method has some disadvantages. First, a lot of scattered wallets, it's uncomfortable. Secondly, for each of them, it is necessary to save a unique key seed-phrase (which will be a private key). So, more digital currencies you have more unique phrases you should remember accordingly. If you lose one of them, then the entire digital currency will be lost from the corresponding wallet.

- Exchange

Many users prefer to store altcoins on stock exchanges. This is very convenient, as trading platforms support hundreds of different alloys. However, please note that you will have to entrust funds to a third party. Most crypto-instruments are centralized, completely uninsured from hacking, and are regularly exposed to DDoS-attacks, which jeopardizes the safety of funds. If you do not trade on crypto-exchanges, then consider other options for long-term storage of crypto-assets, where private key control is provided and, consequently, complete control over digital assets.

- Online Wallets

This option also implies the control of funds by a third party. On the other hand, online wallets often support many popular crypto-currencies and even allow for transactions with low commissions.

- Mobile wallets

Now there are a lot of mobile wallets, both for Android and iOS. Many crypto-currency online services also have a mobile version.

Some mobile wallets are highly reliable (because they allow you to save the seed-phrase) and an intuitive interface. To such applications, it is possible to carry, for example, a mobile wallet Coinomi.

- Clicks in the form of browser extensions

In this segment, Jaxx has gained considerable popularity, existing as extensions for Chrome and Firefox browsers. It features ease of use, minimal design, and flexibility of settings. And, most importantly, it gives you control over the private key in the form of a seed-phrase.

- Desktop wallets

A good tool is a multicurrency wallet, installed on the computer. For example Exodus which features an intuitive and beautiful interface, control over private keys and the built-in exchange platform ShapeShift. At the moment the wallet supports 7 crypto-currencies, including ETH, DASH, LTC, REP, GNT, and DOGE. As for the Jaxx wallet, it also has a desktop version available for Windows, OS X, and Linux.

- Hardware wallets

This type of cryptocurrency can be considered as the most reliable since such devices provide maximum safety, "cold storage" of digital assets in a protected, isolated environment. This is perhaps the best way for long-term storage of significant amounts of funds. A private key is securely embedded in the hardware crypto, which is used to sign transactions. Among the most popular wallets of this type are Ledger Nano S, Trezor and KeepKey. Each of them supports several of the most popular altcoins, including ETH, LTC, DASH, etc.

8.1. Register your wallet and security

Which wallet to choose?

1.	Offline wallet: https://bitcoin.org/ru/choose-your-wallet (ideal for storing large sums for a long time)

2. Coinbase online wallet: https://goo.gl/UFXaio (if you need to send payments occasionally because the exchange can hack and it is not responsible for your funds, it is only suitable if you actively trade)

Security:

1. Turn on Two-Factor Authentication on your online wallet using:

- Google Authenticator, instruction: https://goo.gl/15448V

- For computers: https://goo.gl/ep0xf1

- For Android: https://goo.gl/sbBxn

- For iOS: https://goo.gl/ZeYgVq

2. Encrypt the offline wallet + put the password.

3. Disabling the Internet, installing antivirus software, removing programs with remote access.

4. Printing codes on paper / making a flash drive.

9. How do transactions in the network bitcoin? Why are the funds not credited for a long time?

9.1. The process of sending transactions to Bitcoin

1. Specify the amount and wallet of a recipient and send the transaction for confirmation in the Memory Pool network.

2. The transaction is waiting for a minimum of 3 confirmations (ideally 6 to be 100% sure that the transaction will NOT be canceled) by the miners who need to determine whether the transaction you selected for you is byte + whether your transaction will fit into the existing maximum block in 1 MB.

3. After confirming the transaction by the miners, it is added to the blocked account and your payment of the money is credited to a recipient wallet.

9.2. What affects the speed of delivery of your payment on the Bitcoin network

1. Load of the Memory Pool network (RAM of all networked miners). The more transactions all members send to the network, the greater the total weight of these transactions (the processing speed is lower).

2. Too "heavy" transaction and it just did not fit into the existing block. The size of the transaction can be less if you transferred 1 bitcoin and you transfer the transaction to 1 bitcoin, or more if you were transferred 10 times to 0.1 bitcoins and YOU from them collected 1 bitcoin and conduct the transaction. In the first case, the weight of the outgoing transaction will be less than in the second.

What in the end?

Cryptocurrency sent from a separate wallet may hang and not be confirmed, in which case it is possible to hang funds in the memorial pool for 72 hours, and then there will be a return to the wallet. Sometimes the wallet after the transaction is returned sends it again to the memorial pool.

9.3. How do I know if a transaction is hanging?

1. Checking the status of your transaction: https://blockchain.info/

2. Unverified Transaction List: https://blockchain.info/ru/unconfirmed-transactions

What to do?

1. Before sending the payment, check with the average commission for the network byte and put it a little more (it is better to choose a wallet that supports the ability to set up a commission manually): http://statoshi.info/dashboard/db/fee-estimates

2. Also, you can check this site: https://bitcoinfees.21.co/#delay

3. You can speed up the transaction confirmation for free by adding its hash manually to the Mining Pool (however, they have restrictions on the number of such transactions per day): https://www.viabtc.com/tools/txaccelerator/

4. You can pay for bitcoin transaction acceleration if you are talking about large amounts: https://pushtx.btc.com/#/

5. Wait until the transaction is "forgotten" by the network (usually up to 1 week). It was not included in the block + meme pool was freed. In this case, it's enough to update your wallet and the funds should appear on it.

10. Altcoins - other cryptocurrencies and tokens

In recent years, the number of new cryptocurrencies has grown rapidly, and the oldest ones are increasingly revealing their shortcomings. This suggests that once one of the alternative currencies will shift Bitcoin from the pedestal.

Of course, Bitcoin is now the most popular cryptocurrency, and it was from its appearance that the rapid development of other crypto-currencies began.

The creators of the BTC provided an open code for their creation, which later allowed other teams to create other crypto-currencies on its basis and develop them. Alternative crypto-currencies are called altcoins, each of which has its own scope and features. Here are some examples:

Litecoin is a cryptocurrency created by a former employee of Google Charlie Lee (Charlie Lee) in October 2011 as an "evolving" bitcoin and based on his open source code.

The maximum amount of Litecoin that can be extracted is 84 million (now there are more than 51.7 million units). The algorithm for mining this cryptocurrency is similar to bitcoin. However, the blocks for which the award is paid, in Litecoin are formed four times faster.

Ripple is a crypto currency and a distributed system of payments with open source. It was launched in 2012 to provide instant, safe and practically free (with the scant commission, which is destroyed) financial transactions of any size.

In its essence, XRP is similar to bitcoin: this cryptocurrency is based on mathematical formulas, it is decentralized, and each wallet of the system contains the history of all transactions.

But there are differences. The traditional blockade of Ripple does not use, as in the case of bitcoin. It is impossible to mend this currency: all coins have already been created. They can be bought at exchange offices (converting points) or on stock exchanges.

XRP is recognized by a number of large banks. Some venture capital funds invested in this cryptocurrency.

NEM (XEM) is based on the blockbuster; you can build billions of services, from online stores to decentralized social networks, ending with serious financial structures with decentralization and high-level protection.

XEM rewards those who support the economy, so users can earn coins simply by conducting transactions among themselves. Such a growth model has much more meaning than just mining. This is a revolutionary way to manage the future. They also have plans to create the first cryptocurrency trading platform, there is no analog of eBay but on the blockbuster.

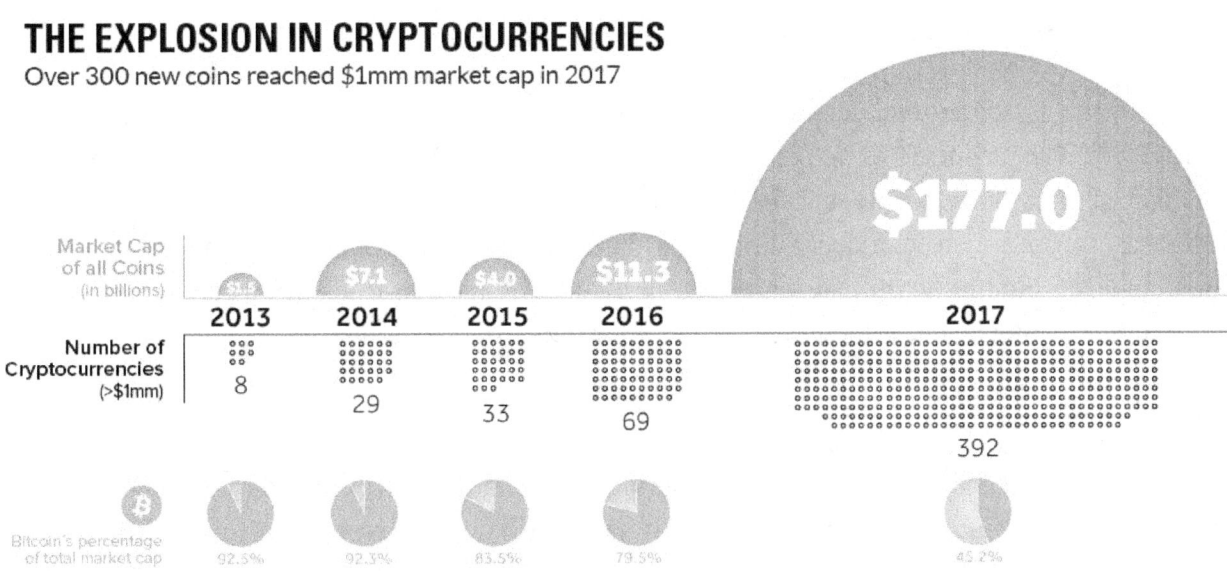

THE EXPLOSION IN CRYPTOCURRENCIES
Over 300 new coins reached $1mm market cap in 2017

What is a token?

A token is an accounting unit that is used to represent a digital balance in a certain asset. Accounting for tokens is maintained in the database on the basis of blocking technology, and access to them is done through special applications using electronic signature schemes.

What are the types of tokens?

- Equity tokens - represent the company's shares.

- Utility tokens - reflect some value within the business model of the online platform (reputation, scores for certain actions, game currency).

- Asset-backed tokens - digital obligations for real goods or services (kilograms of carrots, hours of work of the builder, etc.).

What can be a token provided with?

Directly provided can be only asset-backed tokens. In this case, the token is a digital counterpart of a real (physical) asset or service. For example, one token can be equated to one square meter of living space or the ability to go for one session to a movie theater. The guarantor of the conversion of the token into security is the organization itself, which stores goods or provides services.

What is asset tokenization?

Tokenization is a process of transformation of accounting and asset management, in which each asset is represented in the form of a digital token. The essence of tokenization is the creation of digital analogs for real values with the aim of quickly and safely working with them. For example, a bakery owner creates an electronic accounting system in which he issues digital obligations for rolls - tokens. Having a fairly good reputation, this owner can pre-sell rolls, selling tokens on trading floors on the Internet. In this case, any owner of tokens can come to the bakery and exchange one token for one roll.

What is the main difference between a token and a cryptocurrency?

Unlike cryptocurrencies, tokens can be emitted centrally (under the control of one organization) and decentralized (under the control of a predetermined algorithm). Processing and acceptance of transactions can also be performed centrally (all servers are controlled by one organization). The formation of the price of tokens can depend not only on the balance of supply and demand but also on additional aspects (binding to an external asset, conditional emission rules or remuneration). In addition, unlike the cryptocurrency, the token does not have its own blocking.

How to buy tokens?

Tokens can be purchased through online trading services (exchanges and exchange points), or in personal transactions (the buyer and the seller agree in person). The very process of token trading is identical to the process of trading cryptocurrencies. In addition, issuers of tokens are often embedded in the web pages of their projects the ability to purchase tokens through traditional electronic means of payment.

Where to store the tokens?

In the processes of transfer and storage, tokens are similar to crypto-currencies. To do this, special wallets are used, which realize the storage and processing of keys, as well as the formation and signing of transactions. Typically, these applications are part of the infrastructure of the tokenization platform.

What are the benefits of tokenization?

- Accelerates the trade process, as it does not require the movement of real assets and registration of documents for property rights.

- Increases the security of storage and transfer of accounting transactions on the basis of blocking technology.

- Removes the need to trust intermediaries, since their participation can be described at the level of a smart contract or even they can be excluded from the chain.

- Increases the functionality of the infrastructure, extends the platform by adding additional modules (multi-level authentication, invoicing, regular payments, replenishment cards).

- Improves ease of use, because many of the features of the platform can be integrated into the user interface of the mobile application.

What are the advantages of blockage in the process of tokenization?

- Organization of a reliable database (ensuring verification of the integrity and reliability of data for each next state of the system).

- Decentralization of a point of failure (processing and acceptance of the transaction by a number of independent servers).

- Organization of a reliable audit (full verification of the correctness of the entire history of changes on the platform by the auditor).

What are the risks and problems of tokenization?

- Personal keys of users can be lost or stolen by hackers, which cannot be predicted and insured.

- Ensuring confidentiality in public lockers is a difficult task since for the process of transaction verification their data must be opened.

- The complex task of scaling in a decentralized accounting system, since a decentralized database has a strict bandwidth restriction.

In order not to lose funds invested in altcoins, focus on long-term investments in coins, in which you see the greatest potential, as well as coins showing a positive trend in the market over time. As a rule, such cryptocurrencies have large communities, show high liquidity on exchanges, and their developers are constantly working to improve its functionality.

11. Where to look the rating, capitalization and the current rate of cryptocurrency and tokens.

One of the most frequently asked questions about the cryptocurrency is where to look at the current online course, the capitalization of cryptocurrency, and generally, see the list of all the cryptocurrencies.

Especially for you, we have selected the best services that will help you see the rating of the crypto currency and find out the current price for the altcoin you need.

1. Coinmarketcap

Coinmarketcap allows you to monitor the capitalization of each of the existing cryptocurrencies. Using it on the charts, you can monitor the dynamics and volume of trading of any of the monitored crypto-currencies for different periods of time. To date, the site can monitor 811 cryptocurrencies on different exchanges. For each cryptocurrency or exchange, information is posted from the official sites and leading to them.

Having chosen the interesting cryptocurrency you can visit its official website, learn about exchanges on which it is traded, visit the official forum where you can follow the main discussions and quickly go to its purchase.

Tracking the capitalization of any of the coins, we see how much in dollars (or other currency) today one or another coin is bought, how much was traded in the last 24 hours and what the price is now in USD and BTC. And also see how much the dynamics of trading in percent.

For the convenience of search, we recommend using the "Search Currencies" field.

2. CoinGecko

CoinGecko — this rating, whose goal is to provide a comprehensive overview of the Crypto-currency. Capitalization, of course, is an important parameter of each of them, but it is easy to manipulate. In addition to capitalization, there are many other factors that have an impact on value, the review of which could be useful:

1. The price of a coin

2. The total value of all coins (market cap)

3. Liquidity (trading volume)

4. Number and activity of developers

5. The number and activity of the community

6. Popularity on the Internet

Also, many may be interested in information on the stability of the currency for attacks 51%, so, for example, the cost of equipment necessary to implement this attack in the network Bitcoin is estimated at 540 million dollars.

Using its unique rating methodology, CinGecko offers an alternative version of the world's leading cryptocurrency, which for many may turn out to be a surprise because of significant discrepancies with the classic rating definition only in value.

3. Cryptonator

Cryptonator is primarily a multi-currency wallet. But you can also look at the exchange rates and the value of the currency.

12. How to Choose a Coin for Investing in 2017-2018?

Important criteria (for traders, 1-60 days):

- Capitalization (TOP 100-150 https://coinmarketcap.com/currencies/views/all/)

- Which exchanges are traded on

- Trading volume per day (min 1% of the cost of capitalization)

- Number of coins

- Cost of a coin

- Volatility (constantly jumping the price - you can catch the moment and successfully sell)

- Risk/profit ratio (lower price for the last year / possible profit from the coin, ideally: 1x3 and above)

Secondary criteria (for investors, 60 - 360 days):

- Is the coin on BitcoinTalk alive: https://bitcointalk.org/index.php?board=159.0

- Advantage and technology of the coin

- Website and social networking, attendance and community activity

- News background

- Is it often pumping (pump)

- Seasonality (spring is the best time, summer is calm, autumn is a strong stagnation in all investments, winter is an upswing)

13. Recommendations on trade in cryptocurrency

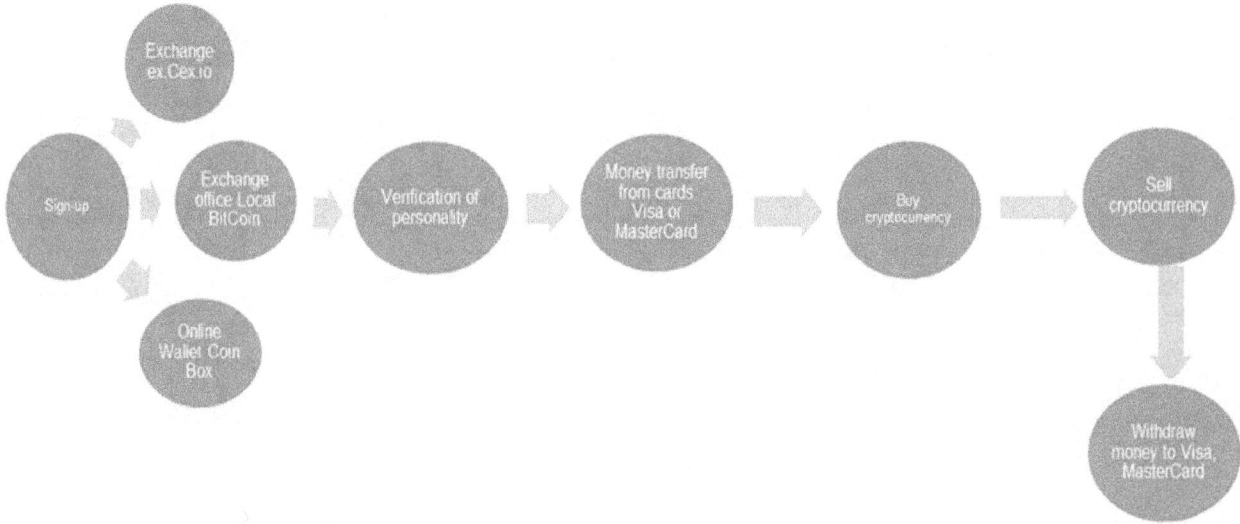

- Never sell the currency below the purchase price to avoid being advised and not to panic, remember that 95% of the market participants experience the same emotions as you do - do the opposite to them, unless of course most points from the Coin Selection Rules are on your side. If not, then it's better to sell out right away. But remember - until you have sold the currency cheaper - nothing is lost yet, it can fly up.

- To fix profit ONLY in bitcoins + to look at growth in PERCENTAGES!

- Taking everything is a bit less risky than doing something one big volume.

- Take on the lower classes, sell on tops. Do not buy on the ups!

- Why it is not worth investing more than 0.1 bitcoins or more than 10% of the deposit - nobody wants a shit-coin and after a pump, they cannot grow for a long time, and you, investing in a large "freeze" your deposit and cannot to trade for a long time.

- Buy on the second long drawdown

- Only 5% of people trade short distances, the bulk keeps and waits, as it does not know how to trade and has lost money on shorts. The faster the currency goes up, the stronger the fall to the bottom.

Short is selling an asset with the expectation that a price will go down. Even if there is no asset available, we borrow it from the exchange and sell it. And then we buy cheaper and we keep the difference between selling and buying.

- It is important to read the news in time and buy coins for pre-emption

- With the growth of bitcoin, altcoin almost always falls, and vice versa (because the capital is being transferred by investors back and forth), so immediately after the collapse of bitcoin, money is transferred to it, and with its rapid growth - transfer to altcoin which most of all sagged and at the beginning of the collapse bitcoin translate everything into dollars, and then repeat the cycle by buying cheaply again bitcoins.

14. The general strategy of investing on the principle of "Hold and Double"

1. Buy bitcoin when the price drops

2. We buy prospective altcoins (those that comply with the recommendations on the criteria for selecting coins, see above) on the second long wave of dropping price

3. We put at least 2 orders/orders for the sale of HALF the purchased cryptocurrency at a price of 2 times higher than the price on the day of purchase (thus the first application we return 100% of your invested funds + half the coins remain on your hands)

4. Part of the returned 100% of funds is left in bitcoins (at least 30%) and the remaining 70% is invested in the purchase of other promising altcoins of the currently falling prices

5. Repeat the process by increasing the deposit and investing in the new altcoins.

15. List of coins in which we invest in late 2017

1. BTC

2. NEM

3. ETC/ETH

4. LTC

5. BCH

6. NEO

7. QTUM

8. BNT

9. OMG

10. CVC

11. 0x

16. What is ICO and how to earn it?

Now, crypto-currencies allow small companies to raise tens of millions of dollars in a short time and start-ups began actively using a new method of raising funds.

In 2017, according to Smith + Crown, during the ICO, $ 180 million was already raised, more than for the entire 2016 ($ 101 million). And the amount of attraction is constantly growing. In the future, according to experts' forecasts, ICO will become one of the most popular ways of raising funds.

Someone talks about the transition to a new economy, the state, and central banks, as always, worry about the issues of control and anonymity, and someone directly points out that many projects that have already passed through ICO have turned out to be fraudulent schemes.

ICO or Initial Coin Offering (the primary location of the tokens) is the issuance of any project coupons or tokens designed to pay for site services in the future - in the form of a cryptocurrency.

ICO works in a similar way with an IPO: investors investing funds get a "share" in the company. The main difference is that under ICO, the investor does not receive the real shares, but becomes the owner of cryptographic tokens, which are traded on crypto-exchanges for the various cryptocurrency. Strictly speaking, tokens are not tied to shares or any other form of ownership.

In this case, ICO has much in common with crowdfunding: in both cases, as a rule, funds are collected for the implementation of a certain concept - that is, at a stage when the company still does not have any product.

The issuing company issues digital tokens and exchanges them for one of the common crypto-currencies, most often Bitcoin or Ethereum. The token gives access to the project after its launch. If the project is successful, people who have invested in it at an early stage will benefit from the increase in the cost of the token.

How to earn?

1. Participate in the bounty program: support the project on their Facebook, Twitter, Bitcointalk accounts.

2. Buy coins in the early stages of ICO, and then sell them more expensive or receive a passive profit from dividends.

Increasing the value of the cryptocurrency is crucial to understanding the essence of the ICO.

Investors buy them not from personal sympathy. These are investments made in the hope of quick and high profits. It is noteworthy that not all crypto-currencies that conduct ICO support their own system of blocking. According to the Smith + Crown research group, some ICOs offer a kind of "meta-token" based on cryptosystems of popular currencies such as bitcoin or ether.

Why invest in tokens issued on ICO

By purchasing tokens issued by the project, investors expect:

- Get the benefit of reselling the tokens at a higher price in the future (assuming they will be in high demand - for example because the project will "fire").

- Use your coupons in the future, having received (as expected) services at a lower price.

- Support an interesting project for yourself.

It is important to remember that the risks for investors are born not only by scammers but also by fairly conscientious companies.

How to find a project for investment and participate in ICO?

You can invest in any project directly on its website, but for this, you need to have a wallet with bitcoins or other cryptocurrency and also be able to carry out transactions. To start a bitcoin wallet it is possible and further, all works approximately as with any system of transfers or the Internet bank.

Information resources on which to find projects that conduct ICO, a lot - Smith & Crown, I CO Alert, TokenMarket, and others.

How to distinguish promising ICO from scam projects (fraudulent)?

Evaluation of the project's prospects is an important point if you want to invest in a project and do not want to lose your money. The following are the criteria for evaluating the project:

1) The team of project creators should demonstrate the necessity and uniqueness of their protocol and token.

2) A professional team and the availability of relevant experience in the declared scope of the project, the absence of a "dark past" of team members

3) A clear roadmap of what will be done when and how, as well as the stages of spending a budget

4) A clear whitepaper with no merging and realistic tasks.

5) Transparent and operational communication between founders and a community.

6) By the time of ICO, either a beta version of the protocol must exist, or it should be used in the test network.

7) It is desirable (with exceptions) so that anyone can get at any time tokens in exchange for resources.

8) When conducting an ICO, the upper limit of the amount of funding must be pre-determined (if the project is launched without a finished product)

9) The project founders' team must own 10% to 50% of all tokens while prohibiting their liquidity during the first 3 years of the project's existence.

10) Attendance at the site, whether everything is done well.

The loudest ICO lately

Although not all primary placements in cryptocurrencies turned out to be successful, nevertheless, the speed of collection and the amount of funds received from the ICO start-ups is amazing.

For the first time in the history of ICO was the Mastercoin project, which in 2013 collected $5 million of investments. The most famous ICO project is the Ethereum cryptocurrency. During its ICO $ 18 million was collected, but then thanks to the popularization of the currency and the growth of its rate, the capital of investors increased by several orders of magnitude.

During the ICO of the Ethereum cryptocurrency project in 2014, one of the most famous cryptocurrencies to date - Ethers (ETH, ethers) was put into circulation. During the ICO, the broadcasts were sold at a price of $ 0.3-0.4 per unit, by July 2015 the price reached $ 20, at the beginning of July the exchange rate of the air exceeded $ 230 per unit of currency, and they are second only to bitcoins in terms of their total capitalization.

In May 2016, the DAO (Decentralized Autonomous Organization), a decentralized investment fund built on Ethereum technology, raised more than $ 150 million during its investment campaign.

Subsequently, hackers were able to use the vulnerability in the DAO code and withdraw from the accounts of the organization about a third of its funds (or about $ 40 million).

Block-start-start EOS is a unique software environment for EOS.IO Software for developing applications based on decentralization. The ICO process of the company takes several stages, and in the first period of placement (June 26 - July 1, 2017) it was possible to raise 651902 ETH, or $ 170 million. The cryptization will end on June 1, 2018. EOS has already entered the top10 by capitalization.

The Texas project, a new blockbuster network called the "Ethereum Killer", launched the ICO process on July 1, and about 2 hours after the start, 2,860 BTC and 2,036 ETH were collected. At the time of writing, the ICO was not yet finalized, but its ICO already surpassed the largest amount of funds raised by the largest crowd scale, Bancor ($ 153 million), and competes with EOS (for $ 185 million).

Many compare the boom of the cryptocurrency markets and the growth of fashion on the ICO with the explosive growth of shares in the Internet industry in 1999 and the accompanying IPOs of dotcoms. This comparison is partly true: like the Internet, crypto-currencies are just a tool. As in the case of Internet companies, many projects that go to the ICO simply try to make money around the new topic. Others, however, offer interesting solutions, which, quite possibly, will change the face of some markets.

17. Where to buy Bitcoin, Ethereum and other cryptocurrencies?

Before you buy bitcoins, an ethereum or other cryptocurrencies you need to create a **wallet** *in which you will store the currency.*

1. Exchange services

There are a large number of exchange services with which you can exchange your dollars from a bank card to a cryptocurrency. They take a commission, but this method of purchase is the simplest. https://localbitcoins.com/

2. Exchanges

The exchange is a platform for trading bitcoins and altcoins. Each participant of the exchange can replenish his internal account and offer others to buy or sell (this is called "order") a certain amount of currency at a certain price. The cost at which users agree to sell or buy bitcoins and make up its course. This course is constantly changing and depends on many factors - even a joke about breaking a cryptocurrency can ruin the cost of bitcoin by several hundred dollars.

The most popular and reliable exchanges are Poloniex, Bittrex and Kraken exchanges. We will talk about them and other crypto-exchanges in the next chapter.

3. Purchase directly

To do this, you need to find someone who wants to sell you bitcoins and negotiate a course, while usually it will be slightly lower than the exchange, because both the seller and the buyer save on commissions. You are the first to transfer the necessary amount of money, in return receive the equivalent in bitcoins. Or do not get it if you fall for the bait of scammers.

Why is it necessary to transfer the first? Because if the seller transfers you bitcoins, and you run away, then he will not have a single chance to return the funds. We strongly do not recommend buying bitcoins from the hands of strangers without checking their reputation.

Currency Exchange

The number of existing crypto-currencies and tokens has long exceeded a thousand. With each new ICO, there is another token. Some of them are rather promising, others have long made a name for themselves, and others are created solely for the sake of quick enrichment of their developers. Altcoin exchanges are also represented on the market in huge quantities so that a novice trader risks completely getting lost in this diversity.

There is a huge number of altcoin exchanges, some of which have nothing to do with fiat money, while others will change the cryptocurrency for dollars. Let's look at the advantages and disadvantages of popular exchanges.

POLONIEX

It is known among traders simply as "Polo", one of the most famous altcoin exchanges, offering a huge number of crypto-currency pairs. It requires two-level verification if the user intends to withdraw amounts above $ 2,000 per day.

Many users criticize the support service of the exchange for its slowness. Also in the community, it was repeatedly noted that the administration of the exchange may be involved in some fraud, primarily related to Ethereum Classic, as well as managed pampas and dumps. But in general, the reputation of Poloniex is quite good and it is the most popular crypto-exchange.

LIQUI

Liqui is a stock exchange based in Kiev with an international team. Unlike most of its colleagues, Liqui proposes the creation of a deposit account, the funds on which are not frozen. To this account, interest is accrued from commissions charged by the exchange. Also, the exchange is marked by a rather tough management style: the administration claims that users will not be contacted about adding altcoins since all such decisions are taken exclusively at the management's discretion.

LIVECOIN

There are a lot of altcoins on the stock exchange, and there is also an opportunity to exchange the cryptocurrency for rubles, dollars, and euros. However, for this, the user will have to say goodbye to anonymity and undergo a special verification. To the pluses of the exchange include the storage of client funds on cold wallets. In addition, users note that the work of the support service is well established on the stock exchange. Nevertheless, many of the listed altcoins have very low liquidity and therefore may present some danger to unsophisticated users of the cryptocurrency.

BITTREX

This American exchange can be of interest to users who put money safety above the user experience. In addition, the Bittrex presents perhaps the largest number of altcoins. Another significant plus of this trading platform is a fairly simple verification procedure, as a result of which it is possible to increase the maximum output per day to 100 BTC. That is much more than we say in Poloniex - the main competitor of Bittrex in the market of altcoins. The shortcomings of the exchange include the slow work of the support service.

Kraken

The Kraken Crypto-Currency Exchange is an Internet platform where several currencies are traded among themselves and to the currencies USD, EUR, and KRW. Here there are several levels of verification, with an increase in the level; you are opened in stages the opportunities for trading, entering and withdrawing the national currency and raising working capital. The entry and withdrawal of national currencies are possible by bank transfer and such transfers as SEPA for EUR, ABA for USD, SWIFT for KRW. A commissions for trade operations account is 0.2% and decrease with increasing working capital. It is possible to use the leverage.

18. Drawing up an investment portfolio and risk assessment

Investment portfolio is an aggregate of prospective assets in percentage of your total deposit.

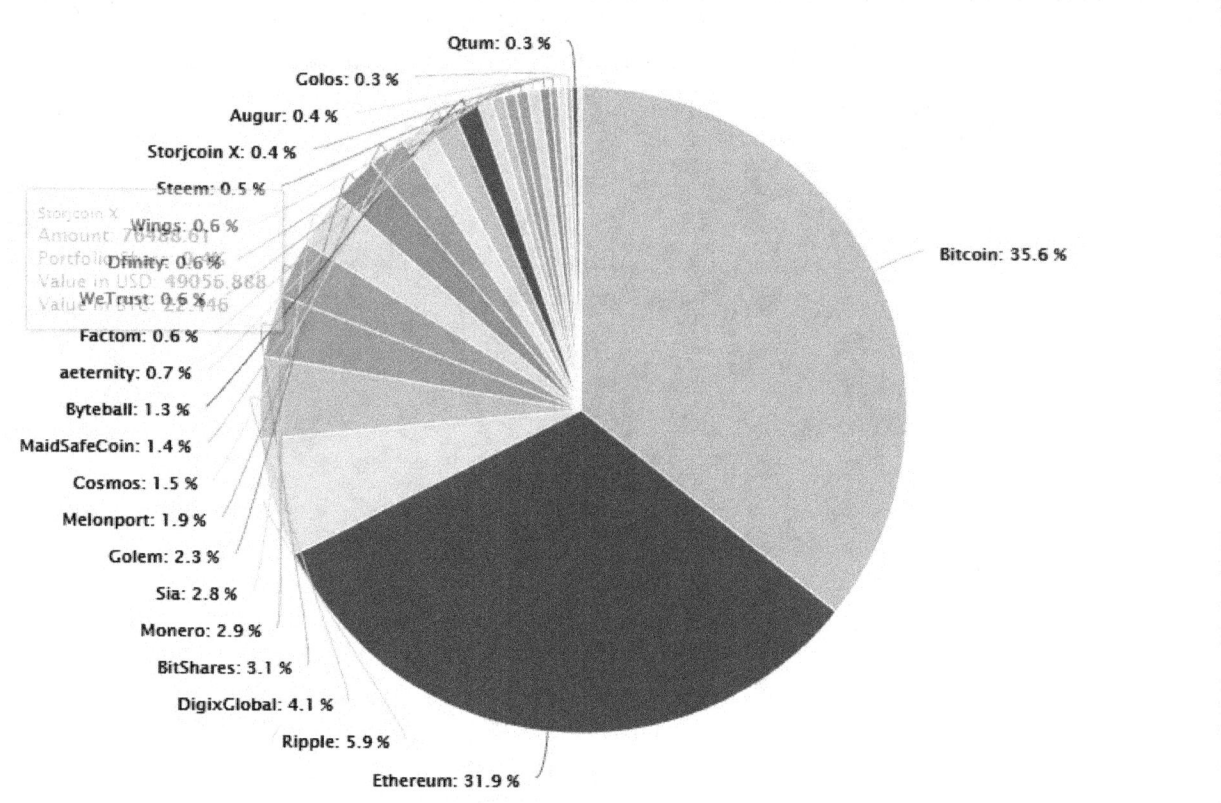

The engines of the market are greed and fear

The investment market is the market for emotions. If growth goes up you are confirmed by greed and there is a temptation to invest everything. If the market has sharply gone down you are overwhelmed by panic and you are frantically selling yourself at a loss.

Trader or investor

Trader - trades for a short distance buying and selling in the range from a couple of hours to a couple of months.

The investor - carefully analyzes an asset and buys it for a year ahead, in the hope of constant growth of the asset.

The trader risks more, but the potential yield is higher.

Margin Trading Margin Trading

Margin Trading Margin Trading (trade through leverage) is the taking on credit of a lack of trade for the creditor against the security of its own funds. In the case of a successful trade you and a lender divide all profit, in case of failure - your funds secured by the lender. Unreasonably risky, do not recommend!

How to reduce risks?

1. Never invest money that you cannot afford to lose.

2. Never borrow money on credit or give important property on bail.

3. Always divide your deposit into different directions.

4. Constantly adjust the portfolio by adding funds to more profitable directions and withdrawing from less profitable ones.

5. Do not buy on tops and do not sell on bottoms!

6. To entrust the management of part of your deposit to trusted specialists: https://www.iconomi.net/

How technically to control your investment portfolio?

1. A pen and a paper

2. A table in Excel

3. Specialized programs, for example, Blockfolio for cryptocurrency

What are Pump and Dump?

Pump is a sharp upward price movement associated with a large volume of asset purchases.

Dump is a sharp price movement downward associated with a large volume of asset sales.

Sometimes pampas can be confused with the news background.

What is the essence?

The asset is bought up sharply, creating the illusion of great demand and introducing novice traders into delusions. Under the pressure of greed, 95% of newcomers are beginning to buy up the asset in the hope of getting rich. When a price reaches a certain point, the organizers of the pampa sharply sell all their assets earning by those who did not manage to sell. There are whole communities where crypto hooligans gather.

What is the benefit for you?

Yes, nothing, at least for you. But they earn you well at a time when you are greedy beginning to buy up the currency that they will pamper. But the reality is that it grows so fast upwards, as it falls down and has time to sell and earn almost unreal. But on you and the other gullible guys will work well and in full.

Services for tracking cryptocurrency from your portfolio

When you start investing in the cryptocurrency, it's important to keep track of the dynamics of the course, as well as your portfolio, and individual coins. Here are 3 best services for easy tracking of the selected coins schedules, dates and prices of purchases and sales and detailed information about each coin.

1. Blockfolio

Blockfolio is a mobile application for Android and iPhone in which you can track information about your crypto-currency portfolio.

Features of the portfolio:

• See all your investments in cryptocurrencies and find detailed information about each coin

• Use notifications to receive notifications immediately when the price crosses a certain threshold

• Candles, warrants and market details for each coin

• More than 800 crypto-currencies, including Bitcoin, Litecoin, Ethereum, Dash, Dogecoin and others.

- View your portfolio in virtually any large fiat currency, including USD, CNY, EUR, GBP, AUD, CAD, SEK, BRL and many others.

2. Cryptocompare

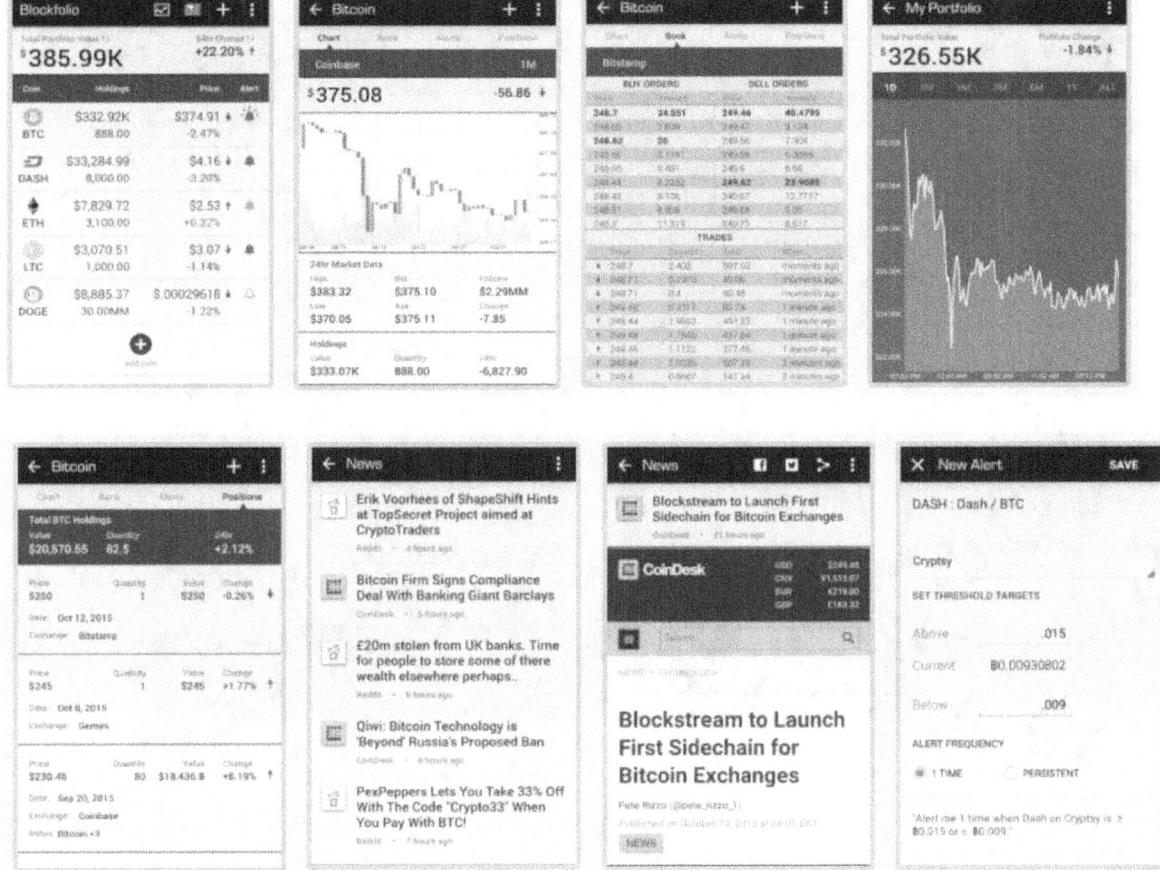

Cryptocompare offers charts, a list of popular coins, as well as monitoring news from various websites.

Just make up your crypto-currency portfolio by adding crypto-currencies. To do this, go to the desired cryptocurrency and click on "+ Portfolio" and in the window that appears, specify the number of bitcoins you have and the purchase price. Also you can leave a comment and indicate which wallet and on which exchange your cryptocurrency is stored.

3. Altpocket

Altpocket is a powerful tool to track your crypto-investment.

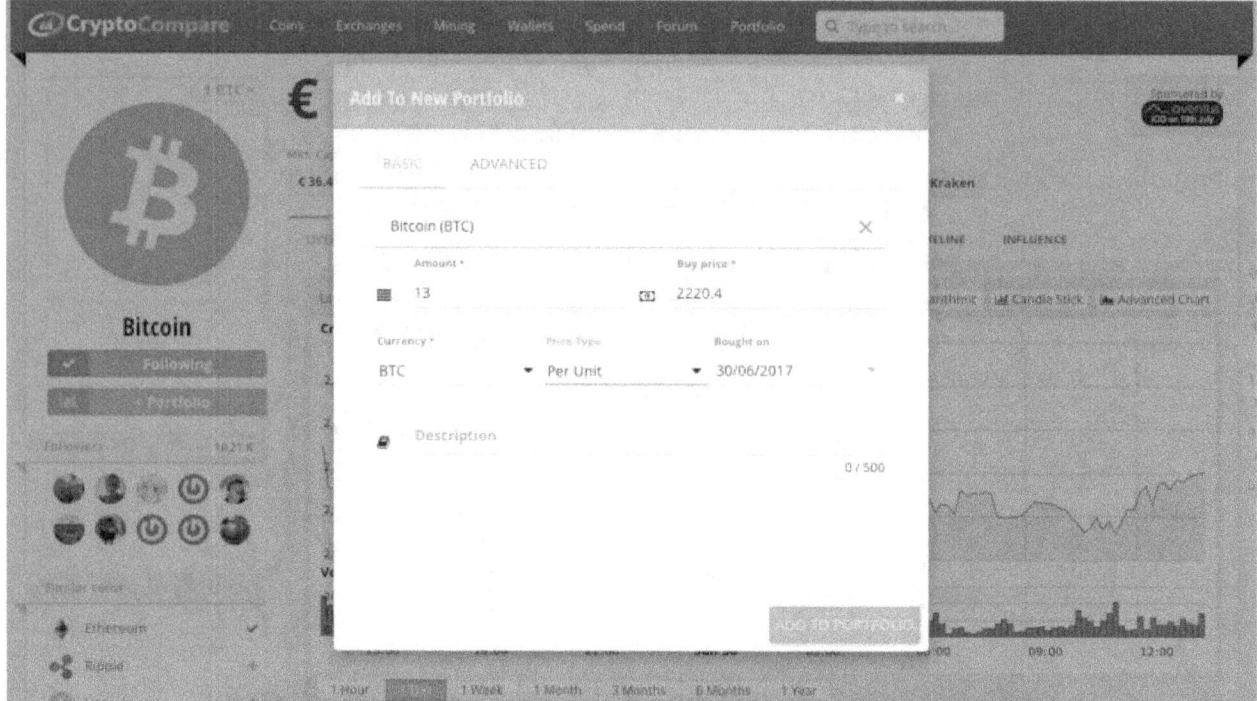

- Professional and easy-to-use tools

- Clean user interface and customizable page your profile

- Supports hundreds of coins

- Currency Implications in BTC or US Dollar

- Automatic capture of investments from Bittrex & Poloniex

19. List of useful services for managing cryptocurrencies

Online wallets:

1. Coinbase для BTC/LTC/ETH Coinbase: https://goo.gl/UFXaio

2. Cryptonator, wallet + store, get $ 10 after a turnover of $ 1000: https://goo.gl/oTvRr9

3. MyEtherWallet: https://www.myetherwallet.com/

4. Holytransaction: https://holytransaction.com/

Offline wallets:

1. Bitcoin Core: https://bitcoin.org

2. Ethereum wallet, Mist: https://ethereum.org/

3. Exodus: https://www.exodus.io/

4. Jaxx: https://jaxx.io/

Physical Wallets:

1. Ledger Nano S: https://www.ledgerwallet.com/products/ledger-nano-s

2. Keeppay: https://www.keepkey.com/

3. Trezor: https://shop.trezor.io/

Other cryptocurrency services:

1. Analysis of all cryptocurrencies: https://coinmarketcap.com/currencies/views/all/

2. Accelerating transactions: https://www.viabtc.com/tools/txaccelerator/

3. Checking the optimal average price per byte in transactions: https://bitcoinfees.21.co/#delay

4. Transfer USD to Satoshi (1 Satoshi is the minimum fractional value of the BitCoin crypto currency, equal to 0.00000001 BTC (bitcoin): https://99bitcoins.com/satoshi-usd-converter/

Analysis ICO:

1. https://tokenmarket.net/ico-calendar

2. http://icorating.com/

3. https://icotracker.net

4. http://www.icocountdown.com

5. https://www.icoalert.com

6. http://happycoin.club/ico-calendar/

7. https://cyber.fund/radar

Popular exchanges:

1. Coinbase: https://goo.gl/UFXaio

2. Kraken: https://www.kraken.com/

3. Bitstamp: https://www.bitstamp.net/

4. Bitfinex: https://www.bitfinex.com

5. Poloniex: https://poloniex.com

6. Bittrex: https://bittrex.com/

7. YoBit: https://yobit.net

8. Livecoin:https://www.livecoin.net/

9. C-cex: https://goo.gl/3y20cM

Drawing up an investment portfolio:

1. The program for drawing up a portfolio on the phone: h https://blockfolio.com/

2. Compiling a portfolio with a PC: https://www.cryptocompare.com/portfolio-public/#/overview

How to draw information:

1. Bitcointalk: https://bitcointalk.org/index.php?board=159.0

2. **Medium:** https://medium.com/search?q=cryptocurrency

3. **Steemit:** https://steemit.com/trending/cryptocurrency

4. **Cointelegrapp:** https://cointelegraph.com/

5. **Twitter:** https://twitter.com/search?q=%23Cryptocurrency&src=tyah